This item is no longer property
of Pima County Public Library
Sale of this item benefited the Librar

This item is no longer property
of Pima County Public Library
Sale of this item benefited the Librar

WWW.HAKSPHOTOS.COM

WWW.HAKSPHOTOS.COM

HAK KAUFFMAN

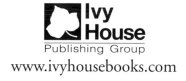

Ivy House
Publishing Group
www.ivyhousebooks.com

PUBLISHED BY IVY HOUSE PUBLISHING GROUP
5122 Bur Oak Circle, Raleigh, NC 27612
United States of America
919-782-0281
www.ivyhousebooks.com

ISBN: 1-57197-467-9
Library of Congress Control Number: 2006903399

© 2006 Hak Kauffman
All rights reserved, which includes the right to reproduce this book or portions thereof in any form
whatsoever except as provided by the U.S. Copyright Law.

Printed in China

To my wife,
Adele,
who has always
supported me
in all my endeavors

I try to create
artistic black and white
photographs for the rational mind
focusing on present day realism.

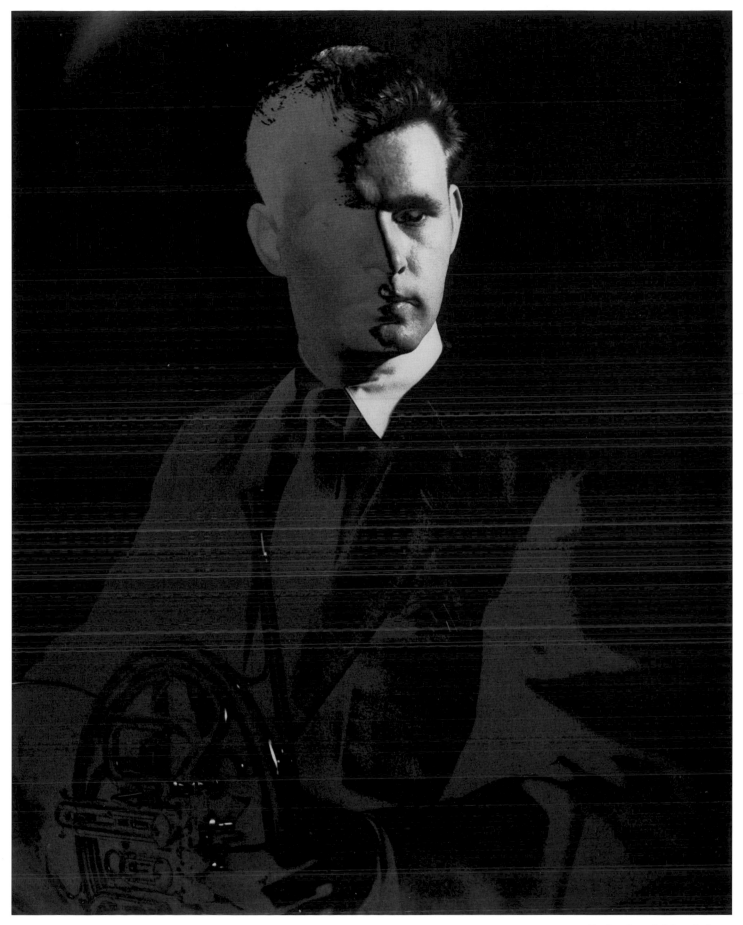

Solarized Musician

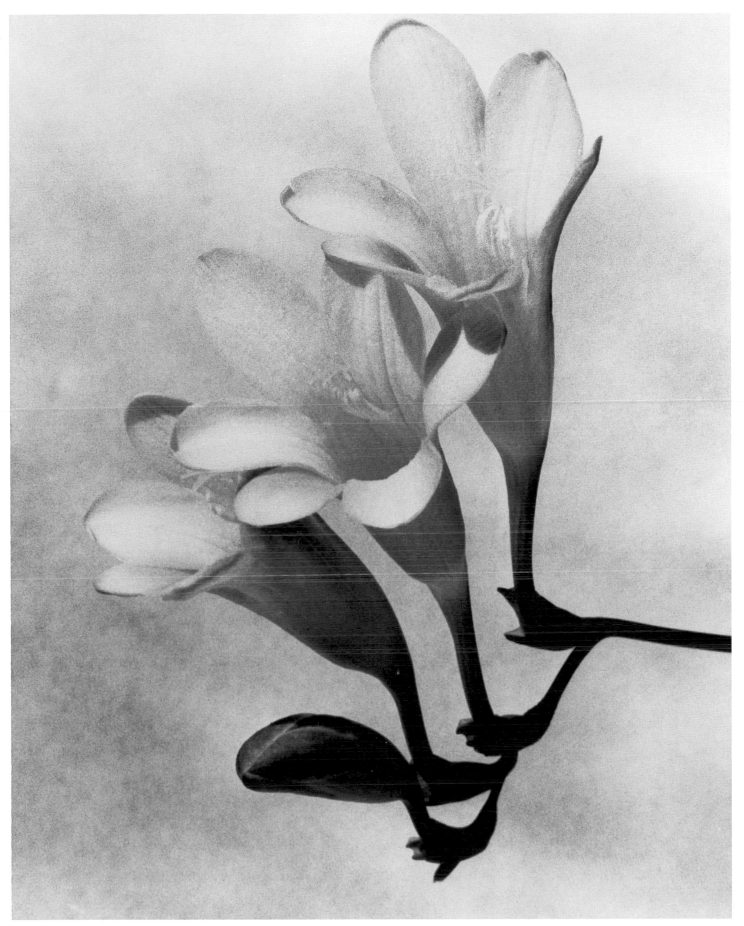

Flower Trumpets

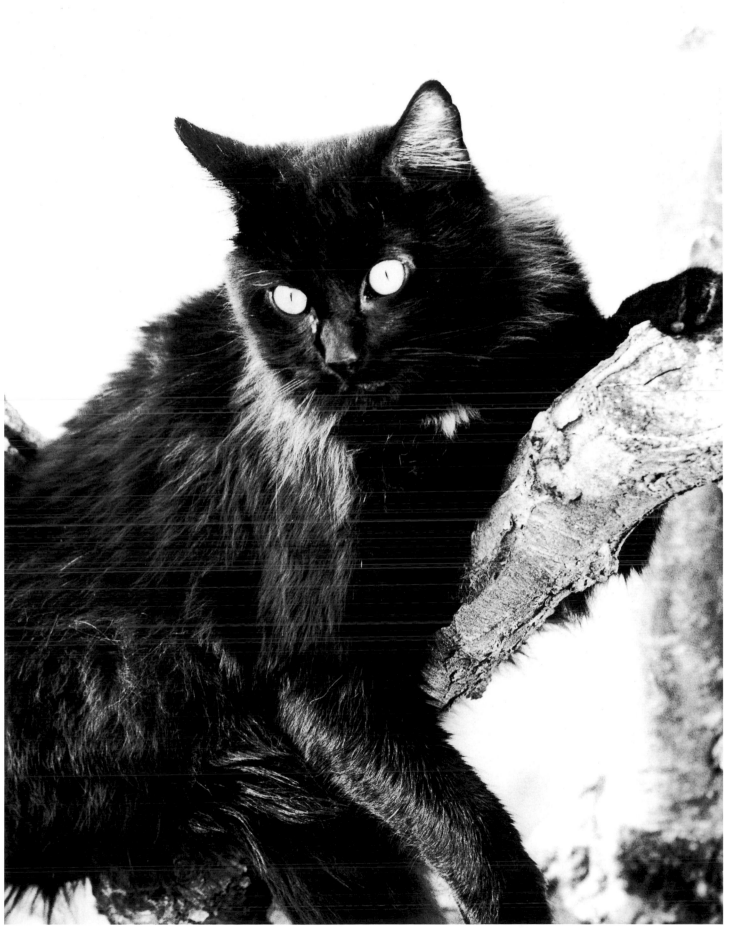

Black Cat

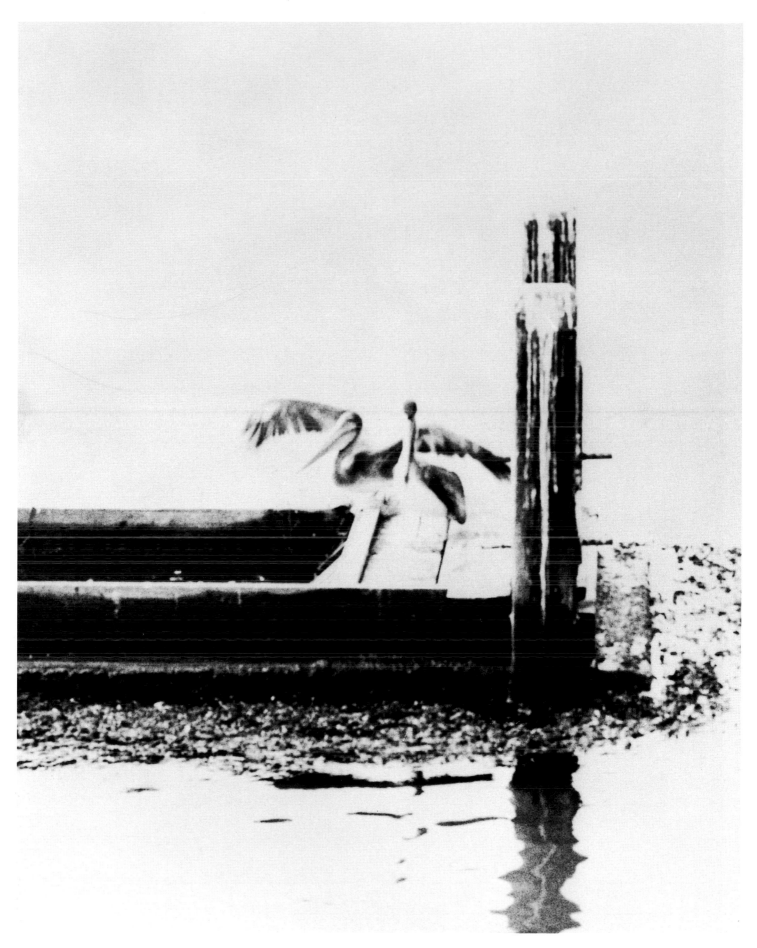

Preflight

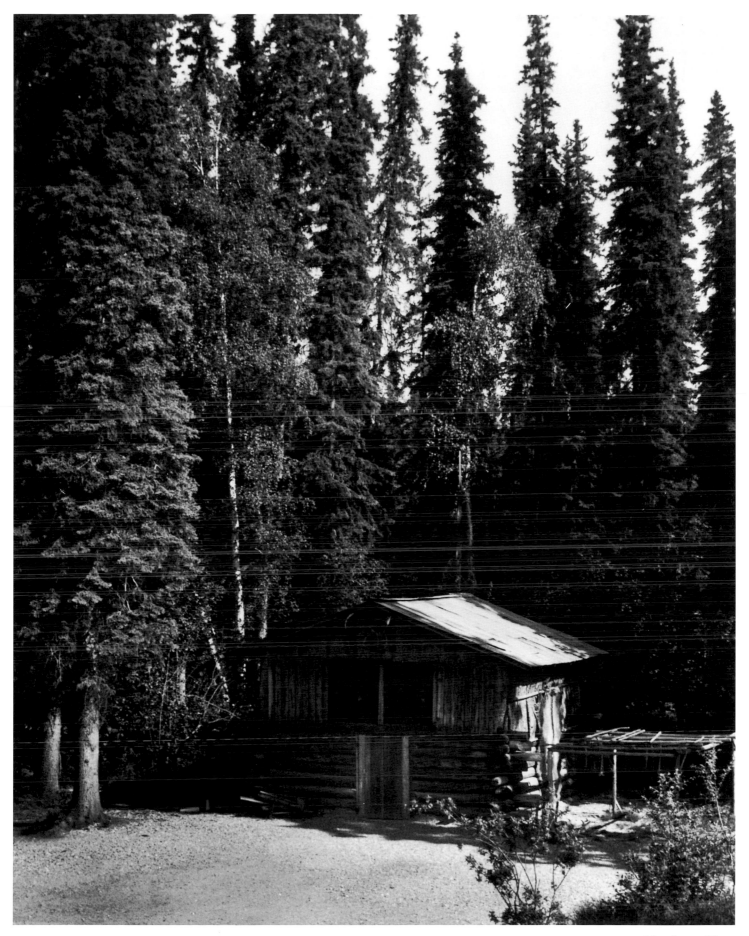

Alaskan Hut

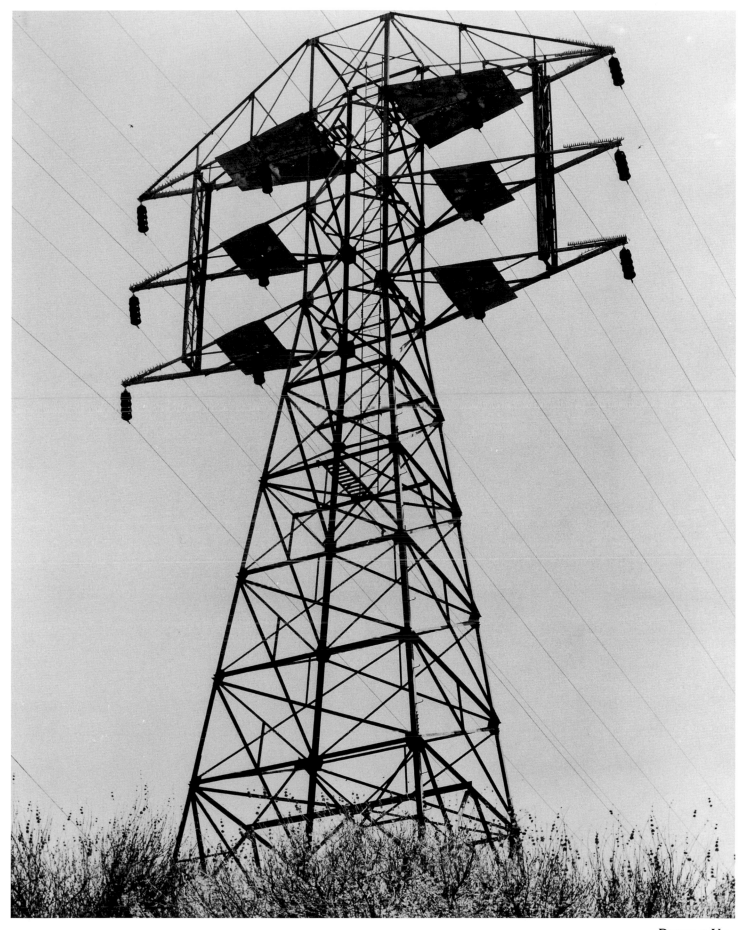

Power Up

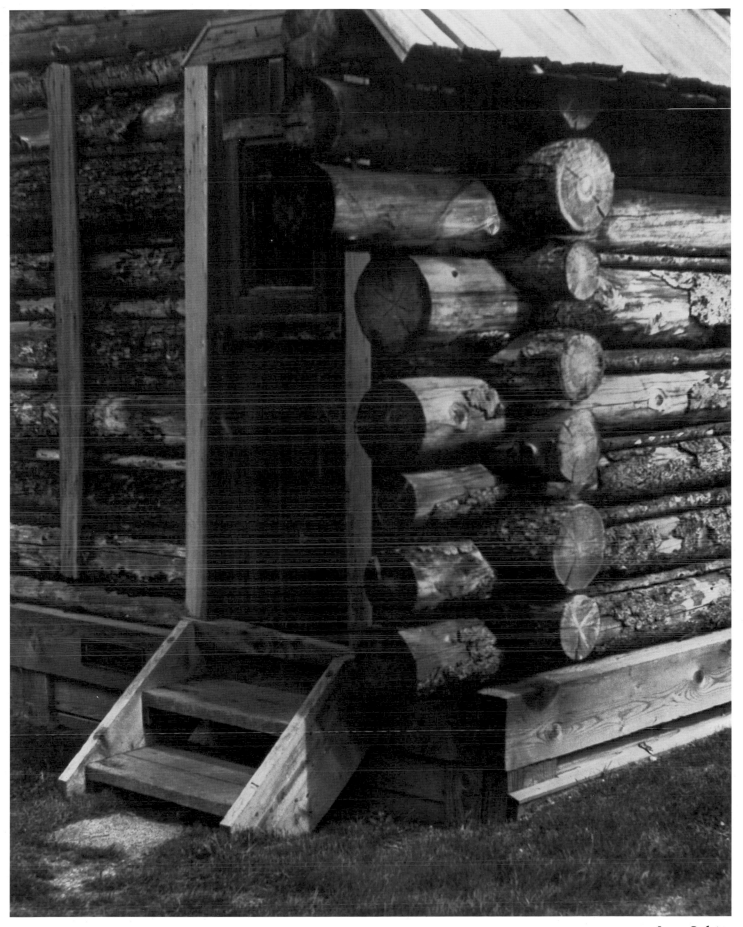

Log Cabin

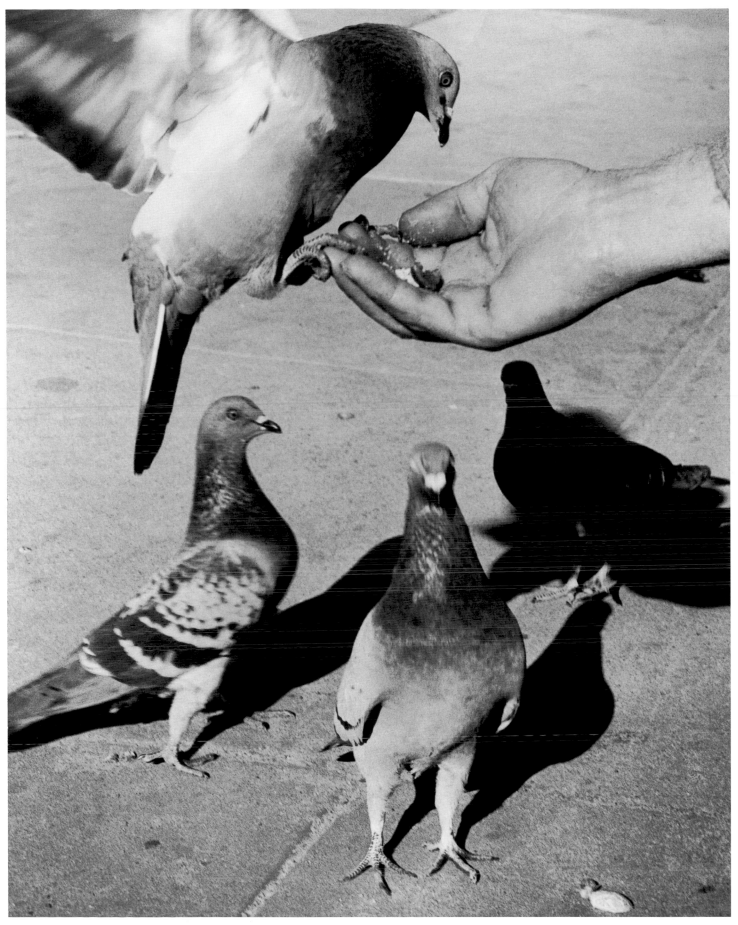

Feeding Time

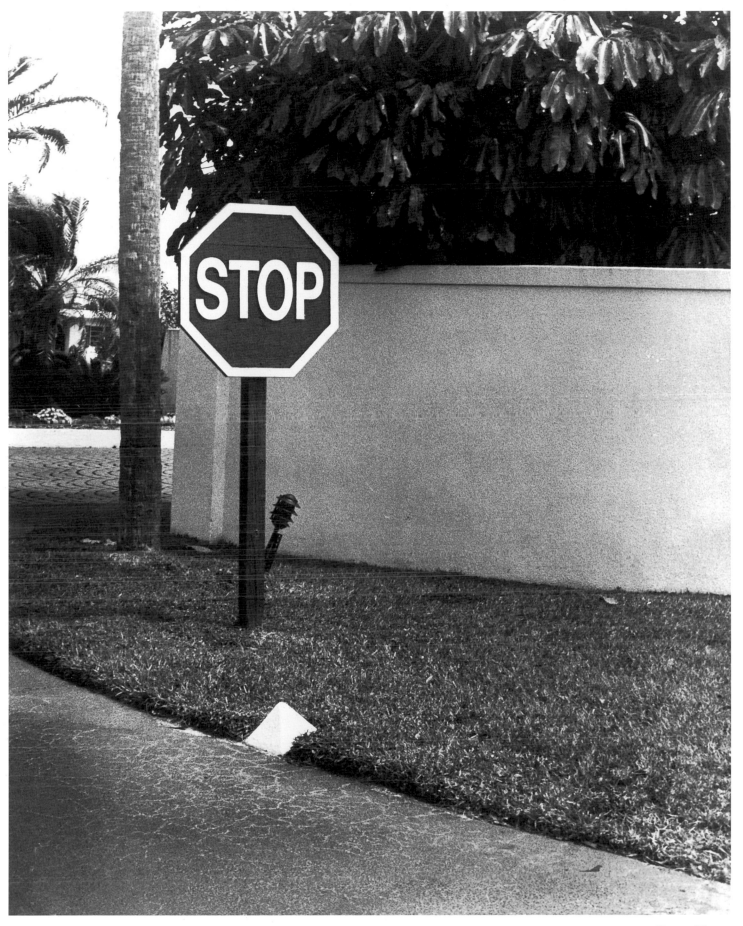

Stop Now

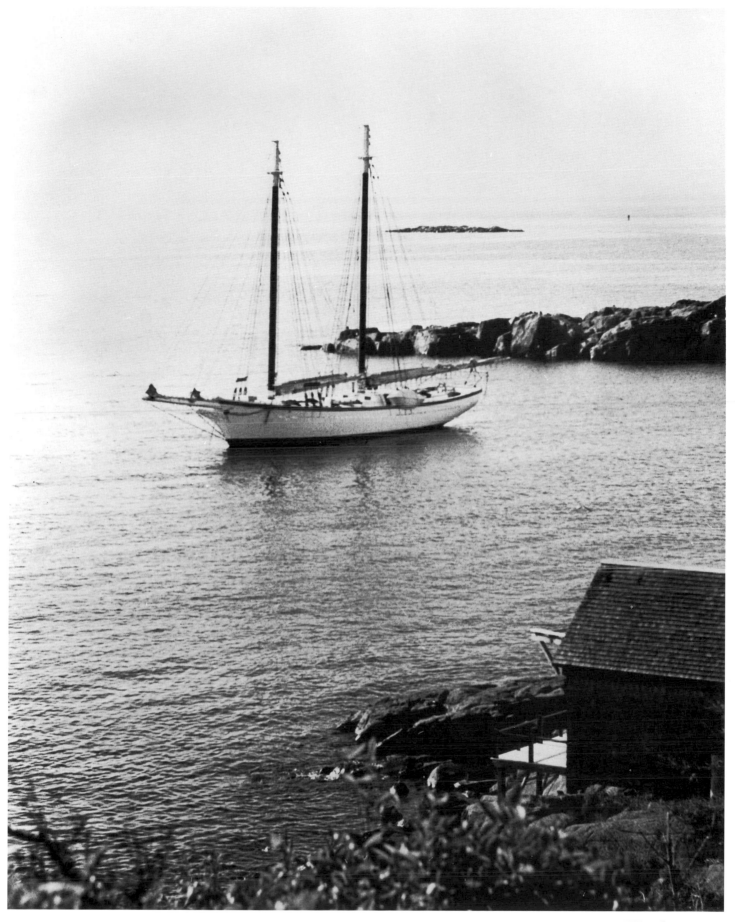

Windjammer

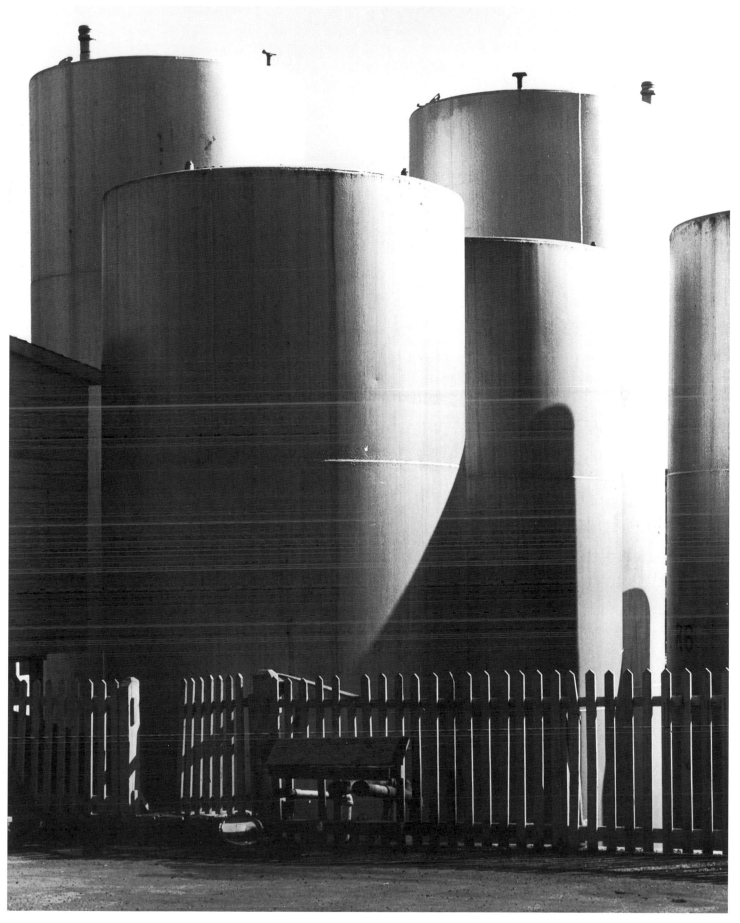

Storage Tanks

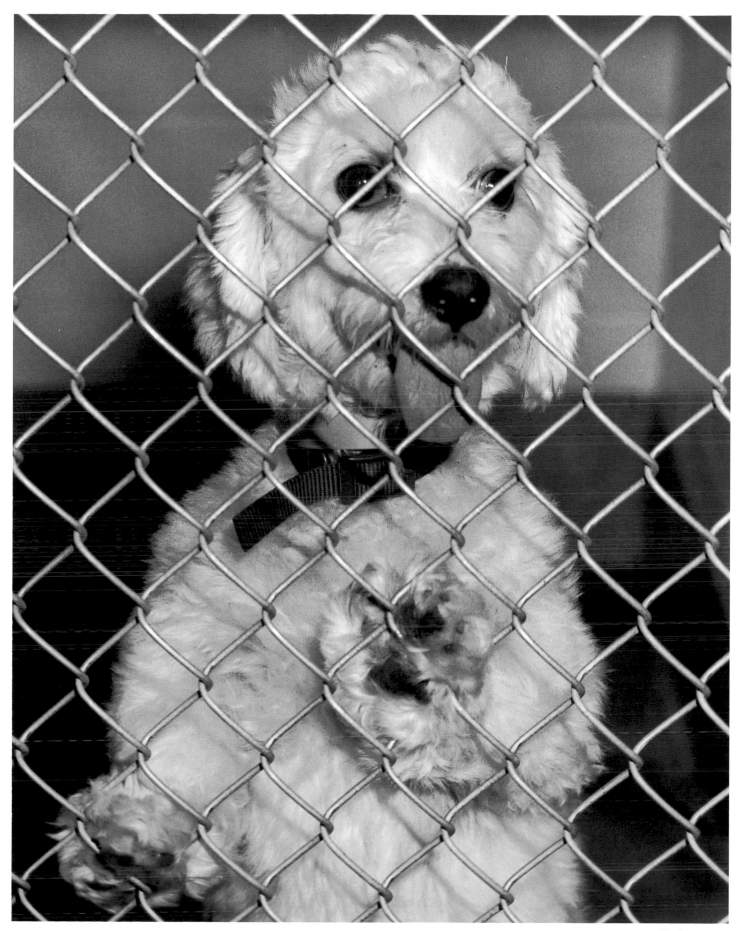

Take Me

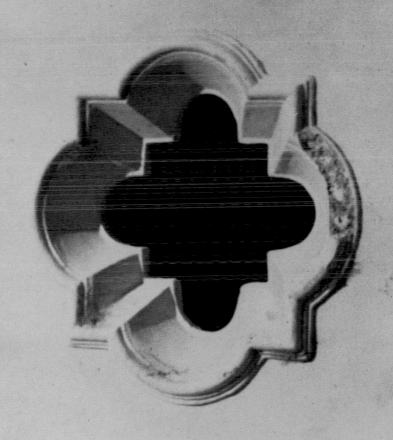

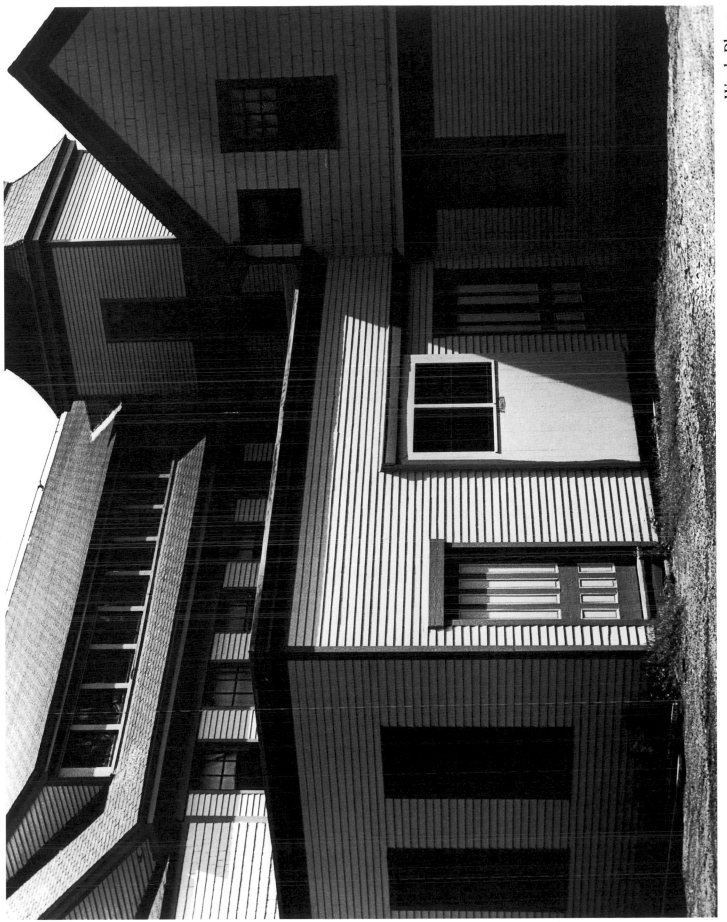

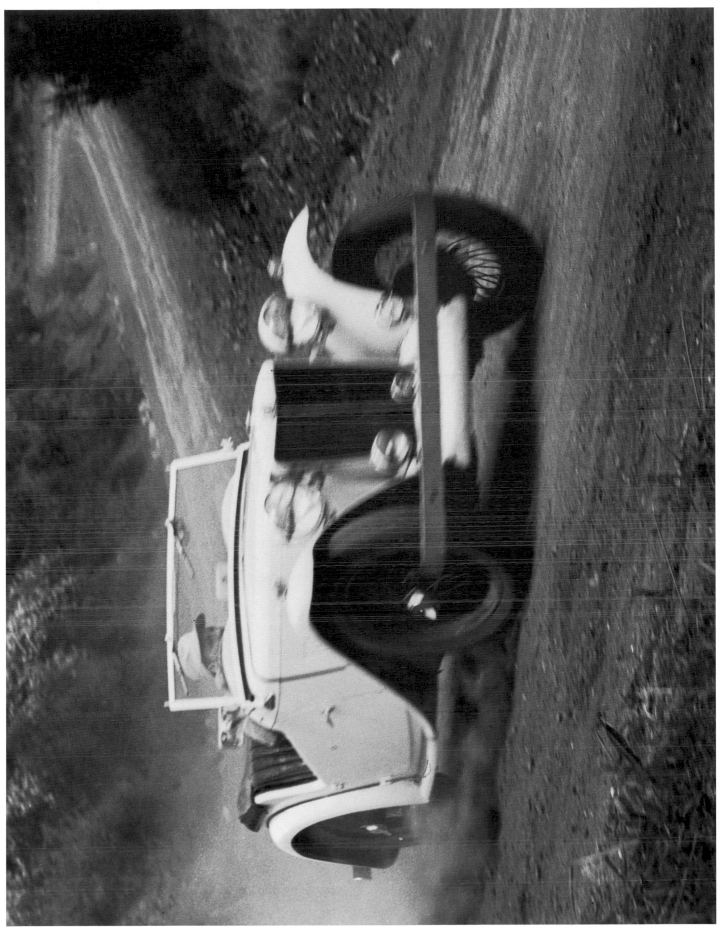

Mr. Pelican

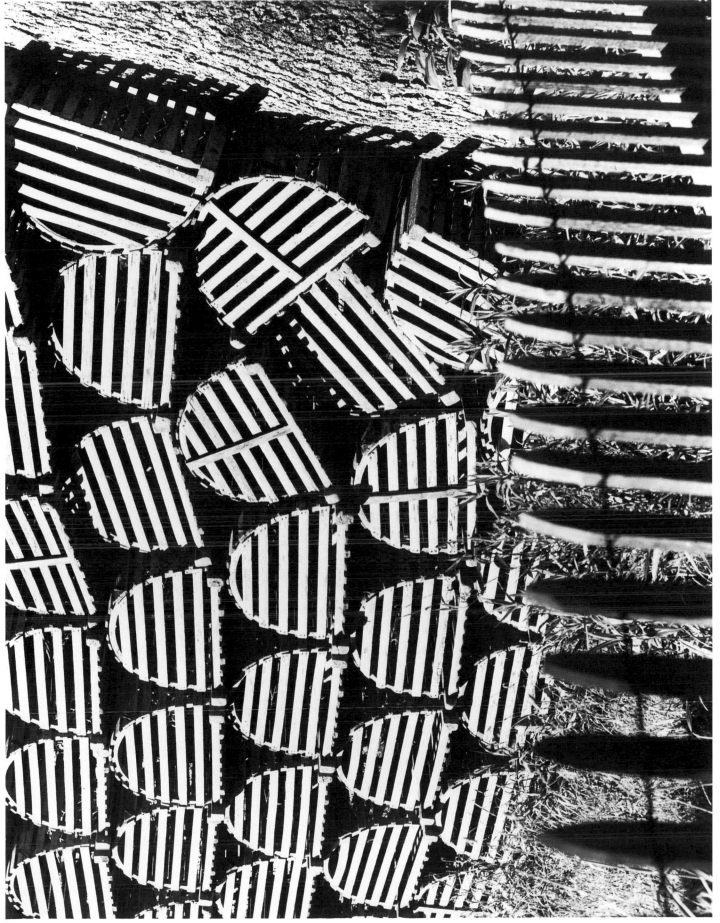

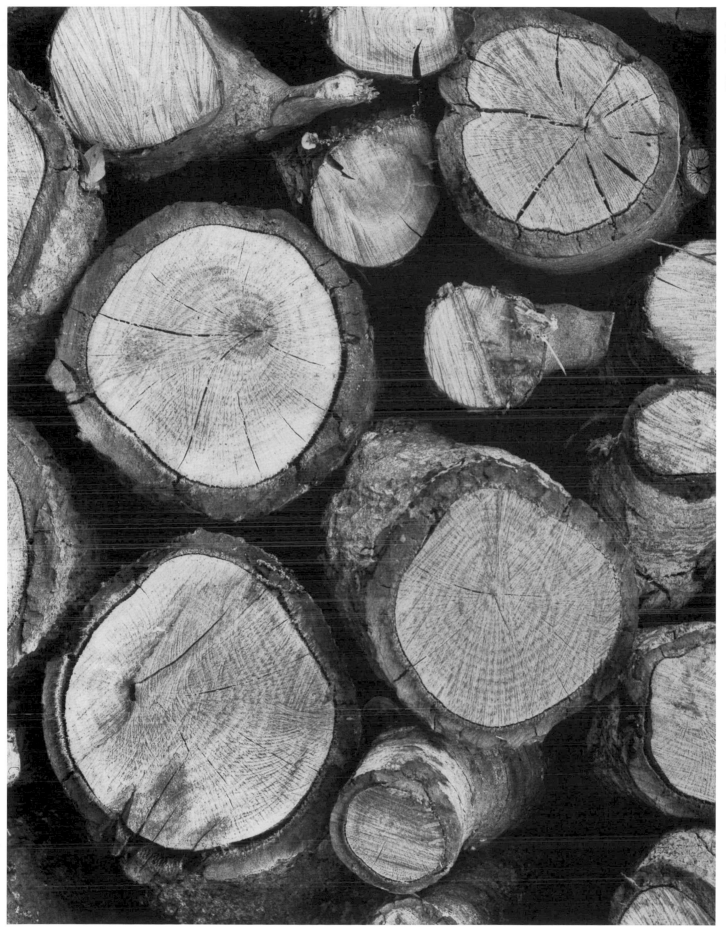

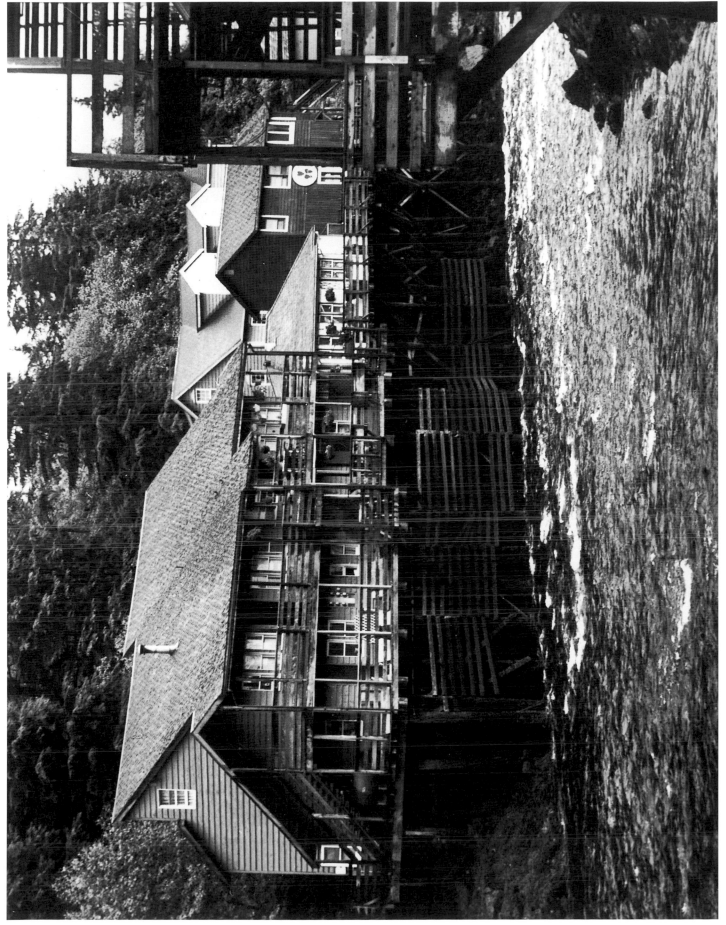

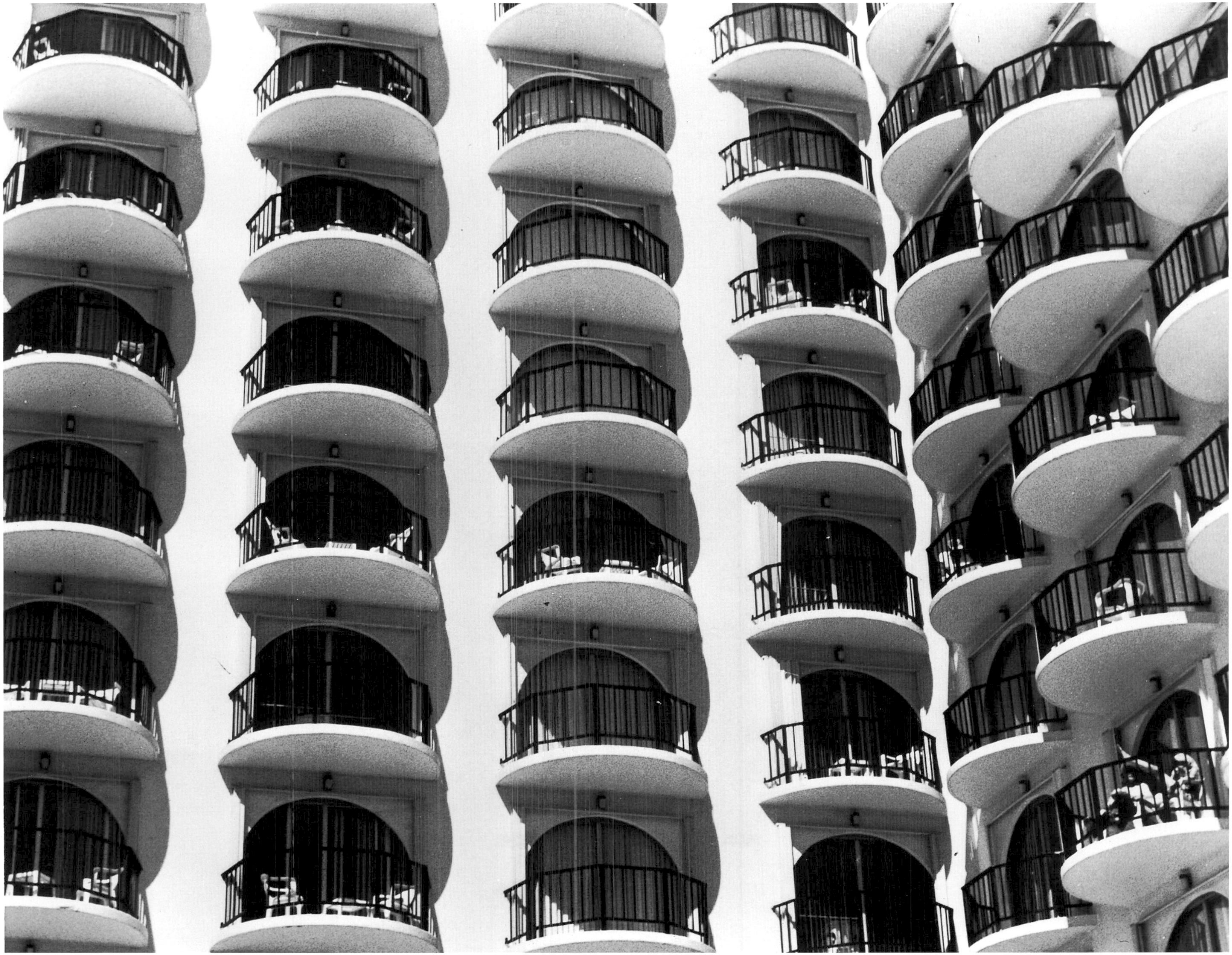

Florida Condo

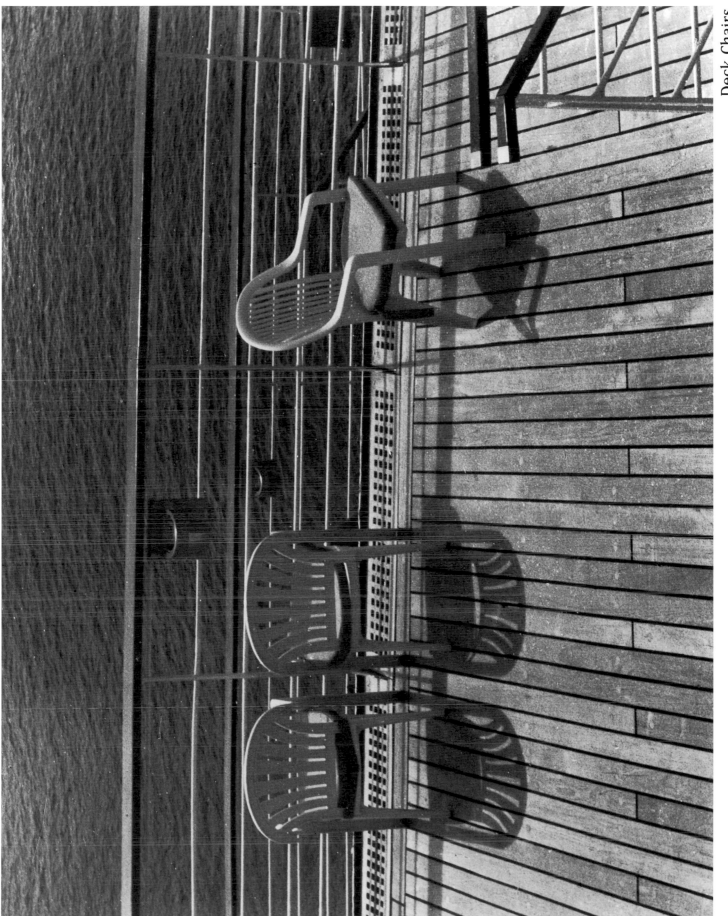

Deck Chairs

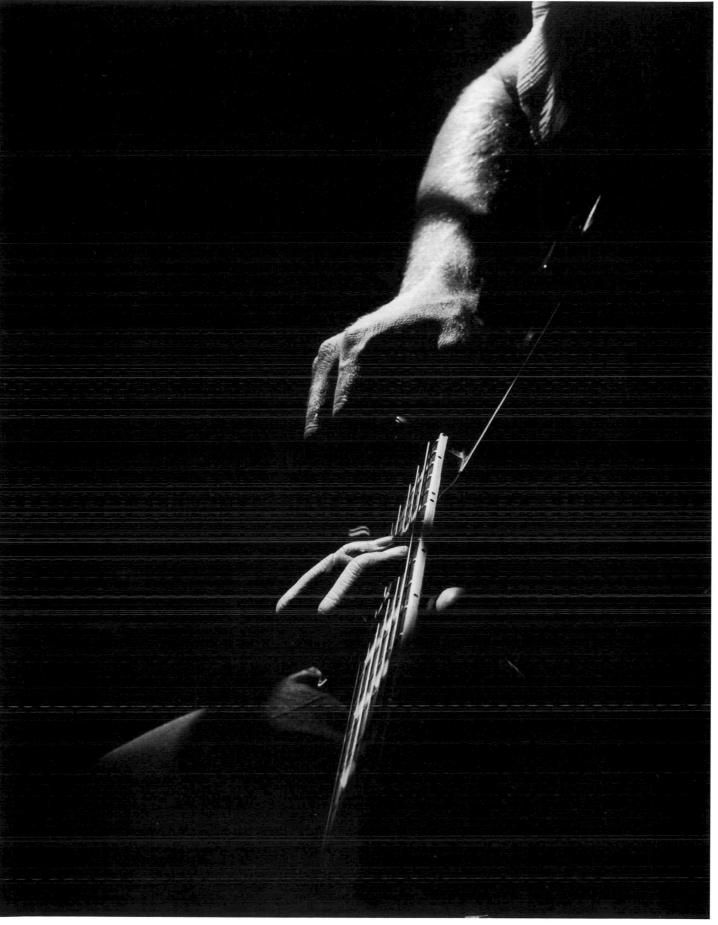

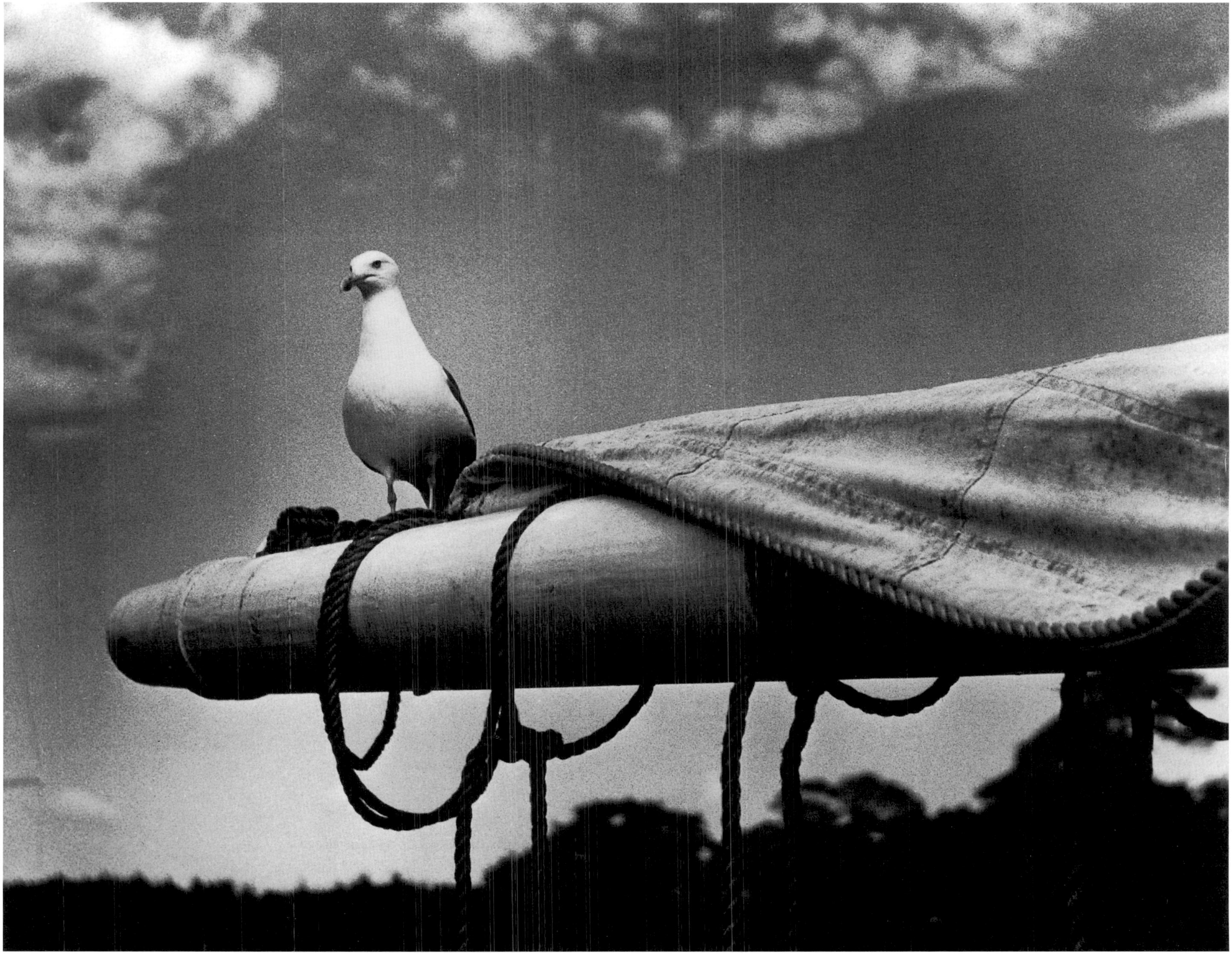

Pretty Seagull

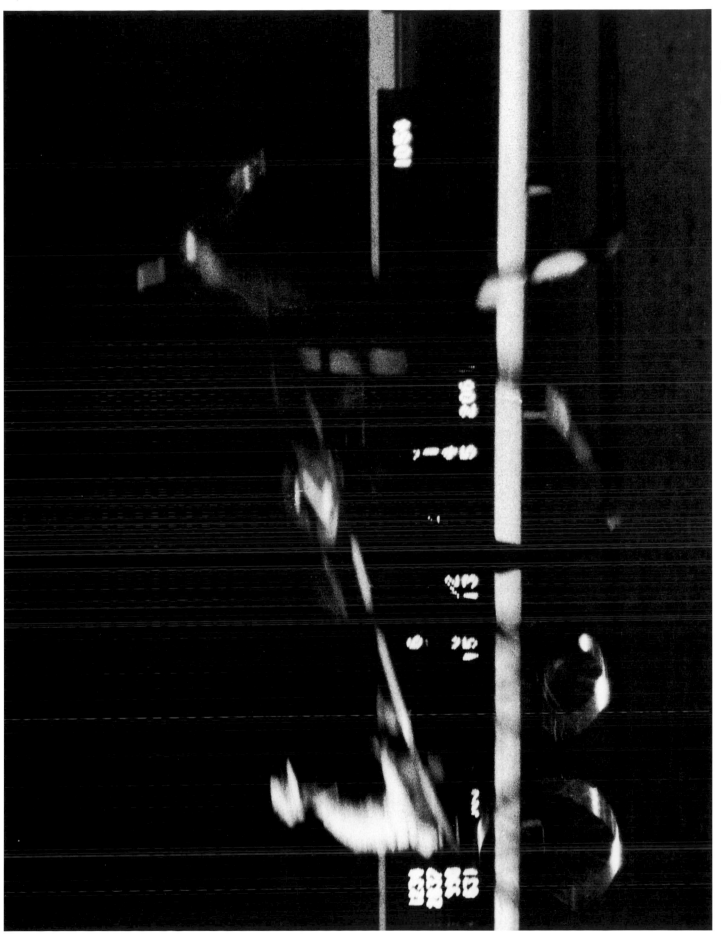

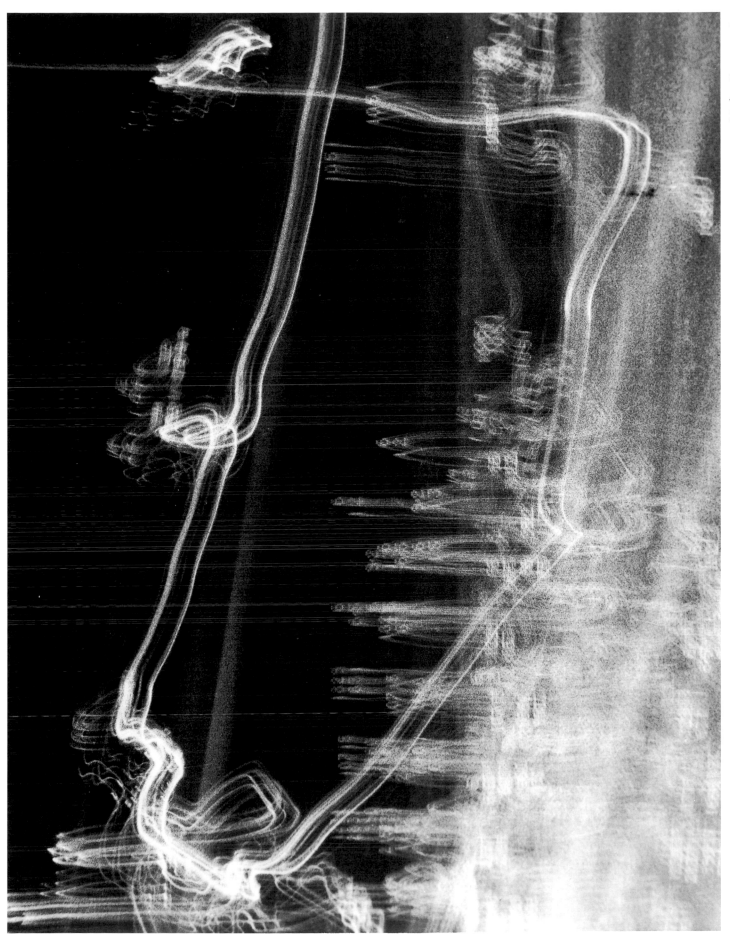

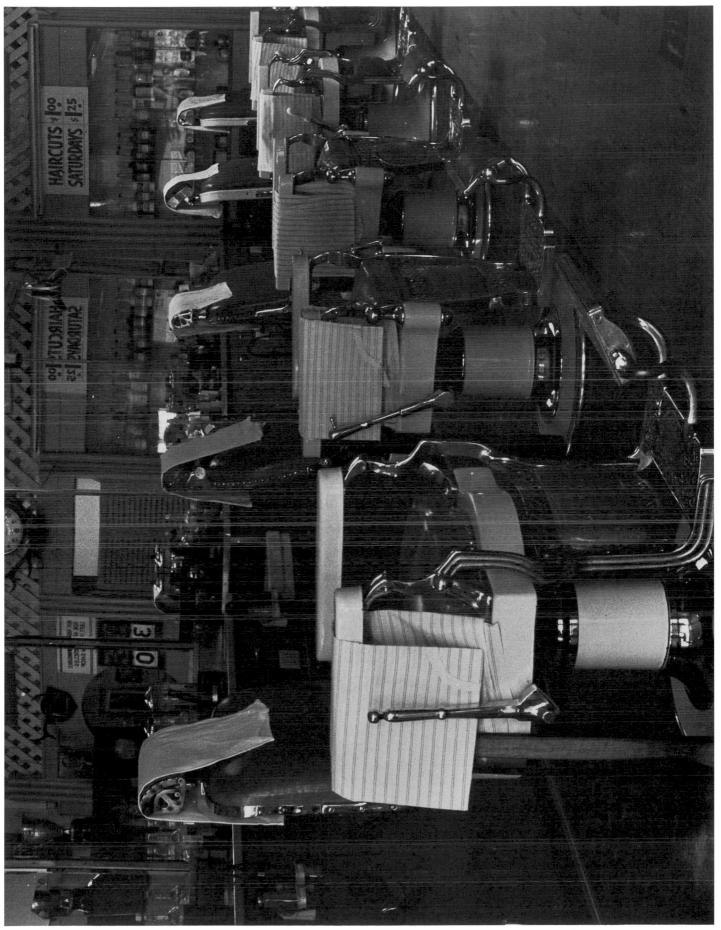

Remember When

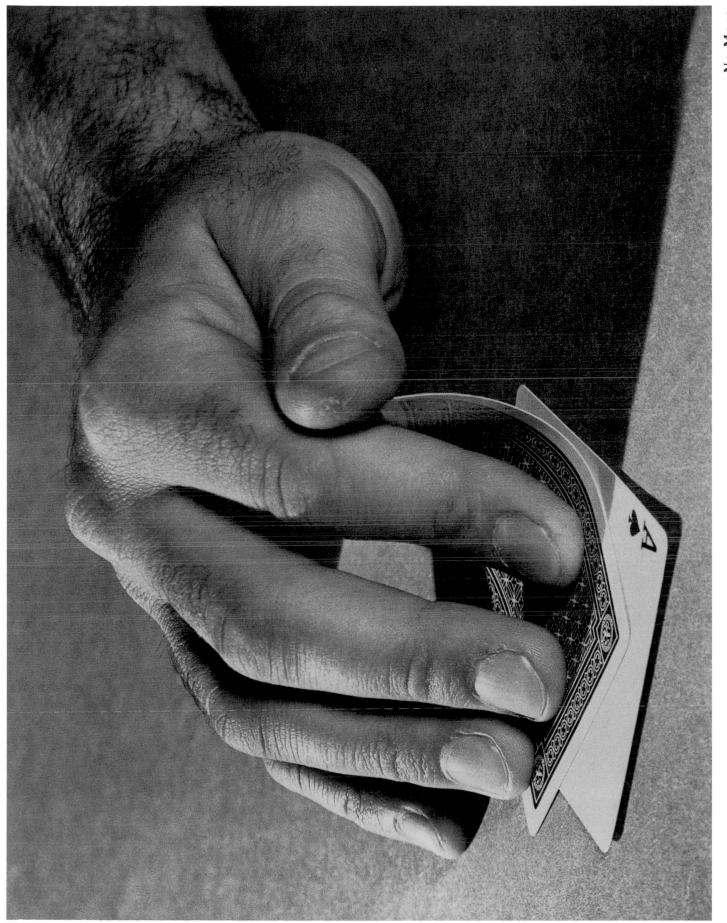

ABOUT THE ARTIST

Hak Kauffman was born on December 5, 1928 and was raised in Philadelphia, Pennsylvania. He graduated from Central High School in 1946 and Temple University in 1950. Kauffman was then drafted for the Korean War in 1951. Following his discharge from the Army Signal Corps in 1953, he attended the world famous Brooks Institute of Photography in Santa Barbara, California. He graduated from Brooks in 1956 and then returned home to Philadelphia, where he easily found a job working for the Standard Photography Studio in center city Philadelphia. One night his father told Hak that he needed help at his wholesale food company. He could not refuse his father, so he had to quit his job and put his love for photography on hold for some time.

After a number of years working for the Jacob Kauffman Wholesale Food Company—where he created the Jay Kay line of packaged food—he notified his brother of his intention to leave and open his own photo studio. But fate had other things in store for him again. Kauffman's brother was murdered during a hold up, so there was no way he could leave. He continued to run the business until he retired and moved to Florida, where he built another photo darkroom. Hak began to exhibit his black and white photographs at local galleries. Then he put some of his photos on his own website. When the idea of a coffee table book showing off his photography began to percolate in his mind, he got up one day and thought, "Why not?" So, here it is. It's yours to enjoy.